Well then—When my Lady was only fifteen she fell deep in love with a fine handsome young fellow, inferior to her both in rank and fortune; but my good old Lord, her father, who doated upon her, was afraid a disappointment might break her heart, and so consented to her having him; but he proved so bad a husband that my poor old Master soon died with grief.

FLORA
Poor man!

JEROME
Don't cry yet, there's something worse to come—My Lady, on this, took such a dislike to her husband, that he died of grief too.

FLORA [Cries]
Indeed, Mr. Jerome, this is very moving.

I0158442

JEROME
On this—

FLORA
I hope there is nothing worse to come?

JEROME
On this, my Lady made a vow to shut herself up from the whole sex.

FLORA
Well, that is more affecting than any of it.

JEROME
And she immediately retired to this lonely castle, where, except the house of Donna Isabella next door, we have not a neighbour for miles; and even there we are strangers—for my part I have never so much as seen Donna Isabella, or exchanged a word with any of the servants since they came to the place—though indeed they have not been here above eight days.

FLORA
But how long has my Lady kept this vow of avoiding all your sex?

JEROME
Eighteen months.

FLORA
Eighteen weeks! what a time!

JEROME
Months.

FLORA
Months! she has certainly lost her senses.

JEROME

Not she.

FLORA

O but I am sure she must have lost some of them.

JEROME

I tell you no.—But I must leave you now, Mrs. Flora, for yonder is Don Antonio, and I believe he is coming this way.

FLORA

I thought no man was admitted into the castle but you, Mr. Jerome?

JEROME

Yes; Don Antonio lives here—but then he is my Lady's uncle; and you know there can be no fear of her falling in love with him, as he is a relation.

FLORA

But you are no relation, Mr. Jerome.

JEROME

Why, as you say, she might fall in love with me—Stranger things have happened—and to tell you the truth, she does not seem positive she shan't, for she bids me keep out of her sight as much as possible, for fear I should put her in mind of that handsome villain that brought her to this retirement.

FLORA

Here comes the old Gentleman!

JEROME

Then I must go, for he'll be wanting to say something to you—he is for ever running after all the maids—I am sorry to leave you—I am, indeed, Flora; indeed I am—Oh it would be a happy thing for me if I could bring myself to care as little for the women, as my Lady does for the men. [Exit Jerome.

FLORA

A fine sweetheart, truly, I have got—and if this old fright proves another, I'll be even with him.

[Enter **ANTONIO**—She courtesys.

ANTONIO

Hah!—what!—what is all this!—what have we here?—what have we here?—a pretty girl—a very pretty girl indeed!—My niece's new maid, I suppose—Aye, aye, I had the other sent about her business—She must be like her mistress forsooth, and have nothing to say to a man—

[Going up to **FLORA**.

My dear, come this way—I think your's is a new face—

FLORA

The Widow's Vow A Farce by Mrs Inchbald

In Two Acts

Elizabeth Simpson was born on 15th October 1753 at Stanningfield, near Bury St Edmunds, Suffolk.

Despite the fact that she suffered from a debilitating stammer she was determined to become an actress.

In April 1772, Elizabeth left, without permission, for London to pursue her chosen career. Although she was successful in obtaining parts her audiences, at first, found it difficult to admire her talents given her speech impediment. However, Elizabeth was diligent and hard-working on attempting to overcome this hurdle. She spent much time concentrating on pronunciation in order to eliminate the stammer. Her acting, although at times stilted, especially in monologues, gained praise for her approach for her well-developed characters.

That same year she married Joseph Inchbald and a few months later they appeared for the first time together on stage in 'King Lear'. The following month they toured Scotland with the West Digges's theatre company. This was to continue for several years.

Completely unexpectedly Joseph died in June 1779. It was now in the years after her husband's death that Elizabeth decided on a new literary path. With no attachments and acting taking up only some of her time she decided to write plays.

Her first play to be performed was 'A Mogul Tale or, The Descent of the Balloon', in 1784, in which she also played the leading female role of Selina. The play was premiered at the Haymarket Theatre.

One of the things that separated Elizabeth from other contemporary playwrights was her ability to translate plays from German and French into English for an audience that was ever-hungry for new works.

Her success as a playwright enabled Elizabeth to support herself and have no need of a husband to support her. Between 1784 and 1805 she had 19 of her comedies, sentimental dramas, and farces (many of them translations from the French) performed at London theatres. She is usually credited as Mrs Inchbald.

Mrs Elizabeth Inchbald died on 1st August 1821 in Kensington, London.

Index of Contents

ACT I
SCENE I - A Hall in a Castle
SCENE II - A Chamber at Donna Isabella's
SCENE III - The Hall in the Castle
ACT II
SCENE I - The Hall in the Castle
SCENE II - A Parlour in the Castle
MRS INCHBALD – A SHORT BIOGRAPHY
MRS INCHBALD – A CONCISE BIBLIOGRAPHY

DRAMATIS PERSONÆ

Don Antonio	Mr. Parsons.
Marquis	Mr. Bannister, jun.
Carlos	Mr. R. Palmer.
Servant	Mr. Lyon.
Jerome	Mr. Edwin.
Countess	Mrs. Bates.
Donna Isabella	Mrs. Riley.
Inis	Miss Brancin.
Ursula	Mrs. Edwin.
Flora	Mrs. Wells.

SCENE: A Village in Spain.

THE WIDOW'S VOW

PROLOGUE

Written by **Mr. HOLCROFT**,

Spoken by **Mr. BANNISTER**, jun.

Prologues, with caustic touch, have often tried
To probe your spleen, prove knaves and fools allied;
Have twisted words and wit ten thousand ways,
To shew that these are most degenerate days!

A different task be ours.—
We'll prove that you
Are wise and happy.
Nay! tho' strange, 'tis true!

First on your safety think! now belles appear
By ample bulwarks guarded, front and rear!
Now male and female amble, side by side,
Exempt from harm, by breast-works fortify'd!
Here polygons defend Miss Molly's breast!
There horn-works hush the husband's fears to rest
By ramparts, daily rais'd, he's freed from cares;
If he'll but grant sufficient for repairs.

Our strength thus prov'd, proceed we to disclose
How new-made wealth thro' new-made channels flows!
How rich we are, in medal-rust and rare things!
In copper coins, gilt pence and—Queen-Anne-farthings!
How shells, stuff'd monkies, and Cremonas old,
In hand of Auctioneer, are current gold!
He "Going! going!" cries. "The hammer's up!
"This fine antique! this Roman—caudle-cup!"
A gem so rare makes connoisseurs turn pale,
Fearful, alike, to purchase or to fail!
Hope trembles, starts, from lip to lip rebounds,
'Till down she's knock'd by—Ah!—one thousand pounds!
The envied purchaser, with joy elate,
Pays for his prize by—selling his estate!
While Smirk, in florid style, words nicely plac'd,
Protests theee lot does, anner to his taste!
[Mimicking]
Yes! sure you're happy! and should rest content,
Now landscapes are reduced fifteen per cent:
And Claude's and Titian's new-found wonders may
By new-made Peers be bought—if new-made Peers can pay.
[Assuming sorrow]
One thing, indeed, may well your peace invade,
Pawnbrokers! threaten you to leave off trade!
[Weeps]
[Returning to his former chearful tone]
All things considered, now, while safety smiles,
And wealth inundates thus our Queen of isles;
While Vickery head defects so soon repairs,
And half unpeoples Greenland of her bears;
While exhibitions, galas and reviews,
Lisle-street, Vauxhall, the Abbey, Handel, Hughes,
Flutes, fiddles, trombos, double-drums, bassoons,
Mara, the speaking-figure, fish-balloons,
Earth-baths, live-eagles, such as never flew,
L'Hercule du Roy! and General Jackoo!
While these create a round of such delight,
Sure, we may hope, you will not frown to-night!

While farces numerous as these go down,
Our farce may in its turn amuse the town;
And, smiling thus on Folly's vast career,
Sure not on us, alone, you'll be severe!

ADVERTISEMENT

The WIDOW's VOW is indebted for the Plot of her Piece, and for the Plot only, to L'Hereuse Erreur, a French Comedy of one Act, by M. PATRAT, but to the Excellence of the English Performers alone is she indebted for its very flattering Success.

ACT I

SCENE I

A Hall in a Castle

Enter **JEROME** and **FLORA**.

FLORA
I Can't go at present, Mr. Jerome, for I expect my Lady every moment to ring, and if I should be out of the way she will be angry; and as I am but new in her service—

JEROME
She angry! Oh you don't know her yet—When you have been a day or two with her you'll find she is never angry—She is the best tempered creature—and were it not for her aversion to us men, she would not have a fault.

FLORA
Do you consider that as a fault, Mr. Jerome?

JEROME
To be sure I do—For my part, I think she had much better be too fond of us, as the rest of her sex are.

FLORA
Pray, Mr. Jerome, what caused her aversion to the men?

JEROME
I'll tell you, Flora, if it wo'nt make you melancholy.

FLORA
Oh, no, Mr. Jerome—I like a melancholy story—I like dearly to cry, when it is not on my own account.

JEROME

Yes, Sir—and I think your's is an old one.

ANTONIO
Hem—hem.—Pray what is your name?

FLORA
A very good name—and I intend never to change it for a bad one.—

ANTONIO
Look in my face—What do you blush for?

FLORA
For you.

ANTONIO
Come, come, no pertness—but let me bid you welcome to the castle.

[Offers to salute her.

FLORA
No, indeed you shan't.

ANTONIO
I will bid you welcome to the castle.

[After a struggle he salutes her.

FLORA
Upon my word, Sir, you are very rude—How would you like I should serve you so?

ANTONIO
Do—Do—serve me so—you are very welcome.

[Enter **JEROME**.

JEROME
Flora, there's a young woman at the gate, who says she lives with Donna Isabella, and wants to speak to you upon some particular business—Can your Honor spare her with no inconvenience to yourself?

ANTONIO
Yes—Yes—she may go—

[Exit **FLORA** and **JEROME**.

A young woman at the gate, now do I want to bid her welcome to the castle—a maid of Donna Isabella, our neighbour—by the bye I must bring about an acquaintance with Donna Isabella and the Countess my niece, if I can, for I am told Isabella is a very beautiful lady—and I should like to bid her welcome to the castle—but, notwithstanding all the pains I have taken, ever since she has arrived, to procure a sight of her, I have not been able—I would, however, force myself into the house, but it seems she has a young brother, the Marquis, come down on a visit to her within these three days, and he might take upon him to resent my gallantry—and I can't say I am fond of resentments, rage and hatred—no, no, the softer passions possess me wholly.

[Exit.

SCENE II

A Chamber at Donna Isabella's

Enter **ISABELLALA** followed by the **MARQUIS**.

MARQUIS
But my dear sister, did not you seduce me to this melancholy spot, on a promise that you would procure me an introduction to the rich widow, the charming Countess?—Interest first prompted my wishes, but since I have beheld her, it is love.

ISABELLA
Beheld her!

MARQUIS
Yes, beheld her—walking in her garden—sitting negligently in an arbor.

ISABELLA
But how?—How contrive to see her?—

MARQUIS
From the top of our house, through a telescope—but, my dear sister, do bring us a little nearer, or I'll purchase a speaking trumpet, and make love to her through it, though my passion be heard by every soul within a quarter of a mile.

ISABELLA
I tell you I have great hopes.

MARQUIS
But why not accept of her acquaintance, and prevail on her yourself to see me?

ISABELLA
I tell you again, the letters I expect from her uncle at Madrid will have more weight than volumes I could say—She dare not disobey him, and must see you.

MARQUIS
And yet I would not compel her to it—Unless she consents to my acquaintance freely, without being constrained by force, or deceived by stratagem, I had rather have recourse to the top of the house and my telescope again.

ISABELLA

Do not let your scrupulous honor overcome all your future prospects—Notwithstanding these letters will strongly recommend you, yet it will be with her own consent only she will yield to the recommendation.

MARQUIS

But when do you expect the letters?

ISABELLA

Every instant—my servants are now gone to the Post office.

MARQUIS

I'll fly and see if they are returned.

ISABELLA

Do; for as soon as the letters are arrived, I would not have you lose a moment but away, and know your fate at once—yet if she will but see you I think with such a person as your's, there can be little to fear.

MARQUIS

But they tell me she is so austere since this rigid vow—so awful—she will petrify me with a look.

ISABELLA

Pshaw—away, and see if the letters are come.

MARQUIS

I will, and if they are, and I gain admittance, I'm resolved I will obtain you a husband within a week, in return, my dear sister, for your kindness to me.

[Exit **MARQUIS**.

[Enter **INIS**.

ISABELLA

Well, Inis—I am impatient to hear—What success?

INIS

Delightful, Madam—I have been introduced to the young Countess—I first communicated the intelligence of the pretended plot forming against her to her waiting-woman, who was sufficiently alarmed at it, to take me to her Lady immediately.

ISABELLA

Well.

INIS

And so, Madam, as soon as I was introduced I fell a crying—I thought that was the best way.

ISABELLA

Very well.

INIS
And then, before I discovered what I had to say, I made her promise not to betray me, which she did most solemnly, and without the least reluctance—and now, Madam, says I, I live servant with your neighbour, Donna Isabella, a flighty Lady, who turns every thing serious and sacred into ridicule; and she has resolved to make sport of you for pretending an aversion to men, and for that purpose she has procured recommendations for you to receive the visits of the young Marquis her brother, but instead of him, she purposes to come herself, disguised as a man, prevail on you to consent to be married to her, and then throw off the mask, and make you and your vow the jest of the whole kingdom.

ISABELLA
This is all right—go on.

INIS
On this she thanked me a thousand times for the discovery.

ISABELLA
But did she say she would receive me?

INIS
Oh yes—she has promised to receive you on my account, that my divulging the scheme may not be detected.

ISABELLA
And she is absolutely resolved to receive me under the title of my brother?

INIS
You may depend upon it—but how are you to proceed now?

ISABELLA
Send my brother to her immediately.

INIS
Your brother!

ISABELLA
Yes—The Countess, from what you have told her, will suppose him a woman, receive him, and consequently suffer a thousand endearing familiarities; till, charmed by the graces of his mind and person, she shall love him without knowing it, and, when she detects the impostor, be unable to part with him.

INIS
And if she is like me, she'll think it the happiest day of her life—but have you prepared your brother how to act his part?

ISABELLA

He has nothing to act, being the very person he represents, and therefore shall not know of the art by which he is introduced—for, except being a little too attentive to dress and etiquette, a circumstance which, with his youthful appearance, favours our design, he is one of the most amiable young men in the world, and the least idea of imposition would shock his honour, and put an end to my scheme.

INIS
Then he is not to know he is to be taken for a woman.

ISABELLA
Certainly not—Hush, here he is, now for my credentials.

[Taking out letters from her pocket.

[Enter **MARQUIS**.

MARQUIS
Oh, my dear sister, there are no letters arrived.

ISABELLA
Yes, here they are—
[Gives a packet of letters]
—my maid has just brought them me.

MARQUIS
O with what joy I receive them—they are all right?—There will be no mistake I hope?—Nothing to make me appear ridiculous?—I would not appear ridiculous for the world.

ISABELLALA
All is right—No, no.

MARQUIS
They are addressed to her uncle!

ISABELLA
Yes, because it will be far more delicate to be introduced through his means—but there is one enclosed to her.

MARQUIS
D'ye think she'll see me?

ISABELLA
Yes; I dare say—There is little doubt of it.

INIS
By my dream last night, I'd lay my life she will.

MARQUIS
Why, what did you dream?

INIS
I dreamt she ordered her servants to drag your Lordship by force out of the house, and duck you in the great fish-pond for a whole hour.

MARQUIS
Is that a sign?—

INIS
O yes—Dreams always go by contraries.

MARQUIS [Going, returns]
But I know she is so haughty and reserved, that, should she admit me, I shall appear confused and awkward.—

INIS
So much the better—she expects you'll be awkward.

MARQUIS
Expects I shall be awkward!

ISABELLA
Pshaw, pshaw—Hesitate no longer with your fears, but away—you know your first court must be to the uncle, and when you have been a little time in the house your apprehensions will vanish.—Away, away.

MARQUIS
But if she should not condescend to see me?

INIS
Oh, my Lord, you may depend upon it she will, because of my dream.

[Exit **MARQUIS** on one side and **ISABELLALA** and **INIS** on the other.

SCENE III

The Hall in the Castle

Enter **FLORA** and **JEROME**.

FLORA
Ha, ha, ha, ha.

JEROME
Ha, ha, ha, ha—But is all this matter of fact?

FLORA

As true as I am alive, Jerome—I have done nothing but laugh ever since I heard it—But do you think, Jerome, she'll be drest all over like a man?

JEROME
To be sure.

FLORA
What, every thing?

JEROME
Yes—Every thing—Egad, I long to have a peep at her!

FLORA
Aye, and so would Antonio too, if he knew.—

JEROME
Aye, that he would—he'd be so fond of the young Marquis there would be no keeping him away from her—but he does not know of it, you say?

FLORA
No; no soul knows of it yet but my Lady and I, and now I have told it to you; and I am to tell it to all the servants as soon as she comes, that they may not think my Lady has broken her vow, by admitting a man—Lord, I wonder how I should look in men's clothes!

JEROME
There's the Priest's old great cloak, doublet, and jack-boots hanging up behind that door, if you have a mind to try, and I'll step out of the way till you have put them on.

[A loud rapping at the door.

FLORA
Here she is—Here she is—Oh dear—Oh dear—how ashamed I am for her.

JEROME [Covering his eyes]
And I wish I may die if so ben't I.

FLORA
And yet somehow I long to see her!

[Another rapping.

FLORA
Run, Jerome, run.

JEROME
This moment—
[Turning back]
—but I am so afraid I shall laugh.

FLORA
O no—Don't laugh—if you do you will spoil all, and my Lady will never forgive you.

JEROME [Looking serious]
Well—I won't—I won't, if I can help it—I'll look so—just so, if I can—as serious as a judge—will that do?

FLORA
Yes; that will do.

[Rapping again.

JEROME [Going]
Ha, ha, ha, ha—I can't help laughing a little though—but not before her—I'll be as serious as a judge before her.
[Aside]
Egad I am afraid—I am afraid I shall laugh.

[Exit, stifling a laugh.

FLORA
Now where shall I run to have a peep at her?—in here.

[Exit **FLORA**.

[Enter **JEROME** bowing before the **MARQUIS** with his face on one side, as if he was afraid to look at him for fear he should laugh.

MARQUIS
Let Don Antonio know I have letters for him.

JEROME
Yes, your Honour—Lordship.

[Lifting up his eyes, looking at him with side glances, and with difficulty stifling a laugh.

Your Honour, your Lordship—Let Don Antonio—know—you—have—letters—for—him.
[Suppressing a laugh.

MARQUIS
Yes; is not that plain?

JEROME
Yes.
[Still suppressing a laugh]
And he'll be very glad to wait upon your Honour.

[Laughs right out and exit.

MARQUIS
A strange fellow this—How my heart beats!

FLORA [From a door]
Oh that she would but turn this way, that I might see her face—Oh the impudent slut.

[Enter **JEROME** with a grin on his face.

JEROME
Noble Lord, Don Antonio will be here immediately.

[Then laughs and stares at him from head to foot.

Here he is.

[Enter **ANTONIO**.

[The **MARQUIS** bows very respectfully whilst **JEROME** is laughing and making faces behind.

MARQUIS
Letters, my Lord, from your brother at Madrid.

ANTONIO
Signior.

[Taking the letters.

MARQUIS [Aside while **ANTONIO** reads]
Heavens, whence this palpitation? If such are the feelings of my bosom on knowing myself in the same house with her, what must be my agitation on a nearer approach!

ANTONIO
My letters inform me it is the Marquis who does me the honour of this visit—My Lord, your Lordship—

JEROME
Ha, ha, ha.

ANTONIO
What's the matter with you?

JEROME
Sir, I was only—

ANTONIO
Only what? Leave the room.

JEROME [Aside]

Well I thought the old Don would have found out a woman in any disguise.
[Exit.

ANTONIO
My Lord, you may command my services and friendship, but I fear you will not rate them so highly as I could wish, as you must be debarred the acquaintance and society of my niece—You are no stranger to the vow she has taken?

MARQUIS
I am not—and yet I flatter myself the manner in which I am spoken of in these letters—

ANTONIO
Be certain, Sir, my niece shall receive them, urged with all my authority for an interview. Will your Lordship take a turn in the garden while I deliver them and enforce their contents?

MARQUIS
I will—and should you prove successful, Don Antonio, I shall ever retain the deepest sense of the obligation.

[Exit **MARQUIS**.

[Enter the **COUNTESS**.

ANTONIO
Niece, I was this moment coming to you, to bring you these letters from your uncle at Madrid, which you will find recommend, in the strongest manner, to your acquaintance, no other than the young Marquis our neighbour—as fine a youth as ever I saw.

COUNTESS
Ha, ha, ha—is he arrived?—

ANTONIO
Now in the house—What is the matter?—Did you hear of his intended visit?

COUNTESS
Yes—Ha, ha, ha—how does he look?

ANTONIO
Delightfully—I don't think I ever saw a handsomer man.

COUNTESS
Man!—Ha, ha, ha, I dare say he looks a little awkward?

ANTONIO
Aukward! No; he is as elegant in his deportment, and as fine, as finished a young fellow as ever I saw.

COUNTESS [After looking over the letter]
Certainly, I shall comply with my uncle's request—Let his Lordship be admitted.

ANTONIO
Niece, I always knew you could not keep your vow—I always knew the very first man that came in your way—crash it would go directly, but let me persuade you to break it by degrees, and not let the world say you made no struggle first.

COUNTESS
Struggle! Now, my dear Uncle, with all your deep discernment, particularly in regard to our sex, to see you at last imposed upon delights me.

ANTONIO
Imposed upon!

COUNTESS
Yes; for this self-same Marquis is a woman.

ANTONIO
A woman!

COUNTESS
Yes; this "fine, elegant creature."

ANTONIO
That is, then, the very reason why I thought her so—"a fine creature,"—now that is intuition, instinct, love without knowing it—But, my dear niece, are you sure you are right? Are you sure you don't deceive me? Don't disappoint me—I can't bear a disappointment in a matter like this—I am vastly pleased, and a disappointment might be fatal.

COUNTESS
I assure you again a woman—sister to the Marquis—and has undertaken this scheme purely to make love to me, and turn me into ridicule.

ANTONIO
Now I think of it again, she was devilish awkward—and I believe wore her sword on the wrong side.

COUNTESS
It is she herself depend upon it.

ANTONIO
To be sure it is—and I'll be hang'd if it did not strike me to be a woman the moment I laid my eyes on her—for she came up to me slipping and sliding, and tossing her head, just as the fine ladies do.
[Mimicks]
Well—But what do you intend to do? I know what I intend to do.

COUNTESS
I shall carry on the scheme, and pretend to be deceived, till I turn the joke she designs for me, on herself.

ANTONIO
Yes; and I intend to have my joke too.

COUNTESS
But you must keep the secret.

ANTONIO
I wo'nt say a word.

COUNTESS
Take his Lordship into the saloon, and I'll wait upon him immediately.

ANTONIO
Aye, my dear—and you need not be in a hurry—Egad, I like the joke of all things.

[Exit.

[Enter **JEROME** and **FLORA**.

FLORA
Dear my Lady, have you seen her?

COUNTESS
Not yet.

FLORA
Well, I declare she looks as like a man!

COUNTESS
I shall certainly laugh in her face.

JEROME
Oh no, don't laugh—Never give your mind to laughing—I did not even smile, but kept my countenance as steady—just thus—Did not I, Flora? Oh—'tis such a weakness to laugh—Look just so—as I do now—

COUNTESS
I must away to the trial, however—come with me to the door, Flora.

JEROME
And be sure you don't laugh—Think on me, and keep your countenance—if you can.

[Exit **COUNTESS** and **FLORA** on one side and **JEROME** on the other.

ACT II

SCENE I

Enter **FLORA**.

Dear me, what a pretty footman she has brought with her!—he made me such a fine bow as I past—and looked so grand—here he is.

[Enter **CARLOS** and bows—She courtesies.

FLORA
O Lord, I hope this is not a woman too! but I dare say it is—
[Aside]
Lord what a pity! but I'll talk to him, and I shall soon be able to find out—and if he does not fall in love with me, I'll conclude it can't be a man.

CARLOS [Aside]
A very pretty girl.
Your humble servant, my dear angel.

FLORA [Aside]
Too conceited for a man.

CARLOS
May I venture, on so slight an acquaintance to protest to you—

FLORA [Aside]
No—he protests—'tis a man.

CARLOS
Permit me to assure you—

FLORA
Sir!

CARLOS
What thus takes up your attention?

FLORA
A doubt I have.

CARLOS
Do you entertain any doubts of me?

FLORA
Yes—Indeed I do.

CARLOS

What are they?

FLORA
I have been trying to put this bunch of ribbons into a right form for my Lady's hair, and I hardly know how.

CARLOS
Let me try.

[She gives the ribbons.

FLORA [Aside]
Now shall I see by the dexterity, whether it is a woman or not.

CARLOS
There—I'll be hanged if I have not done it to a nicety.

[Returns the ribbons.

FLORA [Aside and sighing]
'Tis a woman, pshaw.

CARLOS
Now I must beg a kiss for my pains.

[Kisses her.

FLORA
No—it must be a man.

CARLOS
My charming—

FLORA
For Heaven's sake go about your business, for here comes a fellow-servant of mine.

CARLOS
I am going into the grove, will you come there presently?

FLORA
Yes—perhaps I may—only begone now.

CARLOS
But you'll come?

FLORA
Yes—I think I will.

CARLOS
I shall wait for you.

[Exit.

[Enter **URSULA**.

URSULA
So, Mrs. Flora, I give you joy of your new sweetheart—For shame, for shame, I saw what passed.

FLORA
Lord bless you—it is only a woman.

URSULA
A woman!

FLORA
Aye, in men's clothes, like the master, and so there could be no harm you know.

URSULA
I did not know the servant was a woman too!

FLORA
Why, I am not sure of it—but I thought so when I let him kiss me, and I thought so when I promised to meet him in the grove—and I will e'en go—for I dare say 'tis only a woman.

URSULA
Aye, now I think of it again, I am sure it is not a man—Do you suppose a Lady in disguise, would take a man-servant to attend her?

FLORA
Very true; and I wish, Ursula, you would go instead of me to the grove, for I am so busy just at this time—

URSULA
And yet old Jerome says, and I never knew Jerome mistaken in my life, he says it is a man—however, I am not afraid of him if it is, and I will go instead of you.

FLORA
No, Ursula—I will go after all—for if it should prove a man, and he should behave rude to you, oh! my dear Ursula, I should never be happy, that I did not take it all upon myself.

[Exeunt separately.

SCENE II

A Parlour in the Castle

The **COUNTESS**, the **MARQUIS**, and **DON ANTONIO** discovered sitting.

ANTONIO [Laughing to himself]
And so, my Lord, you once thought of the army—Do you think you should stand your ground in a battle.

MARQUIS [Surprized]
Sir!

ANTONIO [Aside]
Damn me but she has a good leg.

COUNTESS
Your Lordship seems formed for the service of a softer Deity; an occupation less perilous than that of war.

ANTONIO
Aye, that you do.

MARQUIS
Pardon me, Madam, the Deity you allude to, I fear may be yet more fatal, unless you will kindly fight on my side.

ANTONIO
Ha, ha, ha, I can't help laughing to think what a pretty soldier you would make—You look vastly like a soldier to be sure.—Ha, ha, ha.

MARQUIS [Angrily]
Why not, Sir?

ANTONIO
Nay, no offence—Damn me if I should not like to command a whole regiment of you—and I would go upon some new achievements—For instance, say the enemy were Hotten-tots, I would undertake to poison them all by the scent of perfumes from my army—or in case of a repulse, would engage at any time to raise a mist, and escape pursuit, only by commanding every man to shake his head, and discharge the powder.

MARQUIS [Forcing a smile]
Upon my word, Sir, you are very pleasant.

ANTONIO
I am very glad your Lordship thinks so.

[Enter **SERVANT**.

SERVANT [To **ANTONIO**]
Sir, you are wanted by a gentleman in the parlour.

ANTONIO
Pshaw—I'm busy—Who is it?—

[SERVANT whispers.

Well then I must come.

[Exit SERVANT.

My Lord I take my leave for a minute, but I shall soon be back.
[Aside]
How like a man she looks—Impudent hussey.

[Exit.

MARQUIS
Your uncle's behaviour, Madam, has something in it rather extraordinary—I hope I have not in any means offended him?

COUNTESS

I can conceal my knowledge of her no longer.
[Aside]
Oh no, my dear, not at all.

MARQUIS [Aside]
My dear!

COUNTESS
I declare I like you so well—so much better than I expected—I can no longer treat you with cold reserve—Come sit down.

[They sit.

MARQUIS
How kind is this!

[Drawing his chair near to her.

COUNTESS [Looking at him from head to foot]
Ha, ha, ha, ha, ha. I protest I can't help laughing—Ha, ha, ha, ha, ha.

MARQUIS
Ha, ha, ha, ha—I protest no more can I—Sure fate directed me to this heavenly spot, where ceremony has no share in politeness.

COUNTESS

And did you suppose I should use any ceremony with such a sweet, sweet fellow as you?

MARQUIS
Egad, I'll use no ceremony either.
[Aside]
Thus, on my knees, let me pour my thanks.

COUNTESS
Oh you artful creature!

[Stroking his cheek.

MARQUIS
Art! I disclaim it—and so do you.—You are all pure nature.

COUNTESS
Well, I positively do think you one of the cleverest of your whole sex.

MARQUIS
Thank you—Thank you—my dearest creature.

[Kissing her hand.

COUNTESS
So negligent—so easy—not the lead awkward or embarrassed!

MARQUIS
Egad, I think you as little embarrassed to the full.
[Aside]
My dear Madam, your charming society has inspired me.

[Salutes her.

COUNTESS
Now, if you were really a man, what would you deserve for that?

MARQUIS [Astonished]
Madam!

COUNTESS
I say, if you were really a man, what would you deserve for that freedom?

MARQUIS
Really a man! Why?—What?—Don't I look like a man?

COUNTESS

Yes—that you do—and a sweet pretty man—Come, come, don't be frightened—shake hands—I forgive you—forgive you all your impertinence—and, carry the jest as far as you will, I am resolved not to be angry.

MARQUIS
I am very much obliged to you—infinitely obliged to you—I assure you this favour—this honour.—
[Aside]
I don't know what to say—She absolutely puts me out of countenance.

COUNTESS
What confused?—Come, resume your gaiety—Come, come—

MARQUIS [Seizing her]
Come, come, then.

[Enter **DON ANTONIO**.

ANTONIO
Hah!—What! Struggling?

COUNTESS
Oh, Uncle, I have been so ill-used by this Gentleman, that I must beg you will resent his behaviour.

MARQUIS
How!

ANTONIO
Certainly, my dear, if you have been used ill.

COUNTESS [Aside to **ANTONIO**]
Most scandalously—Frighten her a little.

MARQUIS
Upon my honour, Sir—

ANTONIO
Zounds, Sir, my niece is one of the most reserved, prudent young women—and whosoever offers an insult to her, it is my place, and consistent but with my honour, to resent it.—
[Aside]
How white she looks.

MARQUIS
Sir, I shall not draw my sword before the Countess, and therefore I beg you will put up your's.

ANTONIO
And so I will, my poor Lady—I see it has frightened you—Here, Niece, have you any hartshorn or drops at hand—the poor thing is terrified out of her life. Come, come, my poor little creature—Poor thing—Poor rogue.

[He goes up to sooth him, and the **MARQUIS**s gives him a blow.

MARQUIS
Don Antonio, this insolence shall receive the correction it deserves.

[Draws.

COUNTESS [Aside]
She is not in earnest, sure.

ANTONIO
I have received many a blow from a Lady, but never such a one as this!

MARQUIS
Do you dare to call me a Lady again, Sir?

ANTONIO
A Lady, oh no—you are a tyger, a fury—

MARQUIS
I never met with such usage!—Damnation!

ANTONIO
What a profligate she is! I did not think such a word could come out of a woman's mouth!

MARQUIS
How, Sir!—Dare to say that again, and I'll nail you to the wall.

ANTONIO [Retreating]
Why, what is all this about? I won't fight—I only drew my sword to frighten you.

MARQUIS
To frighten me!—Did you think I was to be frightened?

ANTONIO
Why not? You see I am.

MARQUIS
Yes, I see, and scorn you for it.

COUNTESS
Why, Uncle, the tables are fairly turned upon you.

ANTONIO
Yes, Niece, and I'm much obliged to you, for your advice in the business—But you may depend upon it, I shall take care how I attempt to frighten one of your sex again.

[Going.

MARQUIS

Come back, Sir, I insist upon your coming back, and recalling what you have said—I insist upon your begging me pardon for your impertinent insinuation.—

ANTONIO

What insinuation?—That I think you a female?—I am sure there is no offence meant in that—for, when I suppose you a woman, I suppose you what I like better than anything in the world; what I am never happy without; and what I even make myself poor, despised, and ridiculous, in the daily pursuit of.

MARQUIS

And pray, Sir, in what, do I appear like a woman?

ANTONIO

And pray, Sir, in what, does any of our modern coxcombs appear like a man? and yet they don't scruple to call themselves men.

MARQUIS

Then you will not recall your sentiments and beg my pardon?

ANTONIO

Beg your pardon?—No—Yes, yes—Put on your petticoats, and I'll fall at your feet as soon as you please.—

MARQUIS

I'll bear this no longer—Draw.

[**MARQUIS** draws.

ANTONIO

Here Jerome, Jerome, come and defend me, where it would be a dishonour to defend myself.

[Enter **JEROME**.

ANTONIO

See, Jerome, how my life is assailed.

JEROME

Aye, your Honour, I always told you the women would be the death of you at last.

MARQUIS

You too, rascal!—

JEROME

Well, I declare with her sword in her hand, she is as fine a creature as ever I saw!—Oh you audacious minx.

MARQUIS
Scoundrel—

JEROME
Sure, your Honour, she must be the Maid of Orleans.

MARQUIS
I am no maid, Sir.

JEROME
I am sorry for your misfortune.

MARQUIS
Don Antonio, this treatment I suppose you inflict as a just recompence for my presumption in daring to hope for an alliance in your family, spite of the prejudice which I knew the Countess had conceived—I cannot deny the justice of the accusation—I came into her house with the vain hope——

COUNTESS
By no means vain—I am ready to comply, be your hopes what they will.

MARQUIS
Can I believe what you say real?

COUNTESS
Certainly—Were you going to say you hoped to marry me? If you were, call the Priest, and we'll be married immediately.

ANTONIO
Aye, if that is what your Lordship wants, the Priest shall tack you together in five minutes.

MARQUIS
This sudden consent staggers me—I was not prepared for it—one likes a little preparation before marriage as well as before death.

COUNTESS
What! you are cast down—alarmed—want to recant—but I won't let you—You shall marry me—I insist upon it.

MARQUIS
What, directly?

COUNTESS
Yes, directly—I am in a hurry.

MARQUIS
I believe this is mere trifling—Swear you will marry me.

COUNTESS

I do swear.

MARQUIS
You are witness to the oath.

ANTONIO
AND **JEROME**
We are witness.

[Enter **SERVANT** with **DONNA ISABELLA** veiled.

SERVANT
A Lady, Madam, who says she is sister to the Marquis.

COUNTESS
Has the Marquis more sisters than one?

MARQUIS
No.

ANTONIO
Then this, I suppose, is your brother?

JEROME
Aye, in women's clothes—O dear, another fine sight!

COUNTESS
Oh Heavens, if it is a man, take him out of the room or I shall faint.

MARQUIS
Sister Isabella, when I shall relate to you the strange reception I have met with in this house, you will be amazed—but I think you will sincerely rejoice at the final event of my visit, when I tell you it is a solemn promise from this Lady to become my wife.

ISABELLA
I give you joy most unfeignedly.

[Pulls off her veil.

COUNTESS
It is a woman.

ANTONIO
Aye, that it is—Madam, let me bid you welcome to the castle.

[Goes and salutes her.

COUNTESS [To the **MARQUIS**]

Why, what are you—
[After trembling as if much terrified]
—an't you a woman?

ISABELLA
Countess, I knew you never would have consented to have seen the Marquis, had he been introduced into the house as a man, therefore I formed this stratagem, unknown to him, thus to bring you together.

MARQUIS [To the **COUNTESS**]
Do not droop, my dearest wife.

COUNTESS
And are you really the Marquis? What a strange blunder have I made!

MARQUIS
I am the Marquis—and it shall be my future care to banish for ever from your memory, the recollection of that marriage which has been the source of so much woe to you.

ANTONIO
Donna Isabella, we are all infinitely obliged to you for this stratagem, by which you have induced the Countess, innocently to break a vow, which she could not have kept without drawing upon herself both ridicule and melancholy—My dear Niece, depend upon it, there is but one vow a woman is authorized to take.

COUNTESS
And what vow is that one Uncle?

ANTONIO
A vow to LOVE, HONOUR and OBEY.

[Exeunt **OMNES**.

Mrs Inchbald – A Short Biography

Elizabeth Simpson was born on 15th October 1753 at Stanningfield, near Bury St Edmunds, Suffolk. She was the eighth of nine children to John Simpson, a farmer, and his wife, Mary, née Rushbrook. The family were Roman Catholics.

Her brother was educated at school, but Elizabeth, like her sisters, was educated at home. Elizabeth also suffered from a speech impediment, a stammer.

Elizabeth's father had died when she was only eight, leaving her mother to take care of a large family. These were difficult times.

Despite the fact that she suffered from a debilitating stammer she was determined, from a very young age, to become an actress. She had loved theatre from her very first childhood visit.

As a young woman Elizabeth was tall and slender. But this beauty brought with it the many attentions of men. It was double-edged.

Elizabeth had written to the manager of the Norwich Theatre to obtain acting work. He had replied that he would welcome a visit for her to audition. For her young naïve years this seemed like a golden opportunity. However, in 1770 her family forbade her attempt to take on an acting assignment there. They had no such qualms with her brother George, who entered the acting profession.

In April 1772, Elizabeth left, without permission, for London to pursue her chosen career. Although she was successful in obtaining parts her audiences found it difficult to admire her talents given her speech impediment. However, Elizabeth was diligent and hard-working on attempting to overcome this hurdle. She spent much time concentrating on pronunciation in order to eliminate the stammer. She was known to write out the parts she wanted to perform and practice the lines to point of such familiarity that her impediment was banished. Her acting, although at times stilted, especially in monologues, gained praise for her approach, and for her well-developed characters. For the audience she came across as a real person, not just an actor performing a piece. Elizabeth would keenly study the performances of others before she herself performed.

In these early months Elizabeth was young and alone, and reportedly also suffered from the attentions of sexual predators.

In June, merely two months after arriving she accepted an offer of marriage from Joseph Inchbald, a fellow Catholic and actor. They had met before on her previous trips to London, usually to see her brother, George, acting on stage. He had written her several letters proposing marriage which she had declined. But now it seemed the most expedient way to make progress in her career.

By all accounts it was still an odd choice. Joseph was a so-so actor, and at least twice her age as well as being the father of two illegitimate sons. The marriage was to produce no children and was not the happiest of unions.

On 4th September of that year, 1772, Elizabeth and Joseph appeared for the first time together on stage in 'King Lear'. The following month they toured Scotland with the West Digges's theatre company. This was to continue for the next four years.

In 1776 they decided on a change of career and a change of country. They moved to France. Joseph would now learn to paint, and Elizabeth would study French. It was a short-lived disaster. Within a month all their funds were gone and a return to England was necessitated.

They moved to Liverpool, Canterbury and Yorkshire and acted for both the Joseph Younger's company and Tate Wilkinson's company in search of permanency and a recovery from their ill-fortune.

Completely unexpectedly Joseph died in June 1779. Despite her loss Elizabeth continued to perform across the country from Dublin to London and places in between.

In 1780, she joined the Covent Garden Company and played Bellarion in 'Philaster'.

In all Elizabeth's acting career was only moderately successful and lasted some 17 years. However, she appeared in many classical roles as well as new plays such as Hannah Cowley's 'The Belle's Stratagem'. Around the theatre she was known for upholding high moral standards. She later described having to fend off sexual advances from, among others, stage manager James Dodd and theatre manager John Taylor.

It was now in the years after her husband's death that that Elizabeth decided on a new literary path. With no attachments, and acting taking up only some of her time, she decided to write plays.

Her first play to be performed was 'A Mogul Tale or, The Descent of the Balloon', in 1784, in which she also played the leading female role of Selina. The play was premiered at the Haymarket Theatre.

'Lovers' Vows', in 1798, was based on her translation of August von Kotzebues original work and garnered both praise and complements from Jane Austen and was featured as a focus of moral controversy in her novel Mansfield Park. Although Austen's book brought more fame to Elizabeth, 'Lovers' Vows' initially ran for only forty-two nights when originally performed in 1798.

One of the things that separated Elizabeth from other contemporary playwrights was her ability to translate plays from German and French into English and to use them as a foundation. These translations were popular with the public and her talents in bringing the characters to life was instrumental in achieving this.

Her success as a playwright enabled Elizabeth to support herself and not need a new husband to carry out this role. Between 1784 and 1805 she had 19 of her comedies, sentimental dramas, and farces (many of them translations from the French) performed at London theatres, although it is thought she actually wrote between 21 and 23 in total depending on which account you think is most accurate. She is usually credited as Mrs Inchbald.

As well she wrote two novels; 'A Simple Story' was published in 1791 and once referred to as "the most elegant English fiction of the eighteenth century". 'Nature and Art' was published in 1796. Both have been constantly reprinted.

Her four-volume autobiography was destroyed before her death upon the advice of her confessor, but she left a few of her diaries.

In her later years she found time to do a considerable amount of editorial and critical work. In 1805, she decided to try being a theatre critic. This literary excursion, after the praise for her acting and more so for her writing, seemed to be a low point in her achievements. The reception to her work amongst her peer critics was low, one commented upon her ignorance of Shakespeare.

Her career from actress, to playwright and novelist was achieved in difficult times for women to accomplish such things. Indeed, whilst the theatre and its boundaries were quite strict she managed, in her novels, to explore political radicalism. Her good looks together with her passionate and fiery nature attracted a string of admirers but she never re-married. Despite her love of independence, she still desired and sought social respectability.

Mrs Elizabeth Inchbald died on 1st August 1821 in Kensington, London.

She is buried in the churchyard of St Mary Abbots. On her gravestone is written, "Whose writings will be cherished while truth, simplicity, and feelings, command public admiration."

Mrs Inchbald – A Concise Bibliography

Plays
Mogul Tale; or, The Descent of the Balloon (1784)
Appearance is against Them (1785)
I'll Tell you What (1785)
The Widow's Vow (1786)
The Midnight Hour (1787)
Such Things Are (1787)
All on a Summer's Day (1787)
Animal Magnetism (c1788)
The Child of Nature (1788)
The Married Man (1789)
Next Door Neighbours (1791)
Everyone has his Fault (1793)
To Marry, or not to Marry (1793)
The Wedding Day (1794)
Wives as They Were and Maids as They Are (1797)
Lovers' Vows (1798)
The Wise Man of the East (1799)
The Massacre (1792 (not performed)
A Case of Conscience (published 1833)
The Ancient Law (not performed)
The Hue and Cry (unpublished)
Young Men and Old Women (Lovers No Conjurers) (adaptation of Le Méchant; unpublished)

Novels

A Simple Story (1791)
Nature and Art (1796)

www.ingramcontent.com/pod-product-compliance
Lightning Source LLC
Chambersburg PA
CBHW021948040426
42448CB00008B/1301